TIME SCRAPBOOK

Contents

Straight from the Tiger's Mouth!

North American Apache (U. S.)
The British call it "The Mustang"

Bell Airacobra
U. S. and British designation

Lockheed P-38 Interceptor (U. S.)
The British call it "The Lightning"

LIQUID-COOLED AI

Endpapers: Colorful war gum cards showing battles, fighters planes, war heroes and homefront activities got kids involved in the war.

AMERICA'S WAR
From Pearl Harbor to V-J Day

Compiled by
*Charles A. Numark &
Martin S. Jacobs*

WESTERN UNION CABLEGRAM

Introduction

America's Wartime Scrapbook – From Pearl Harbor to V-J Day offers a fascinating look at a time of great fortitude, emotion and patriotism. When America entered World War II, it joined Europe in being involved in the war effort in every imaginable way. From the soldiers, sailors, airmen and marines fighting in the mud, water and in the air to the housewives building aircraft and the kids collecting scrap, America's war machine had been roused into action. Like it or not, we were at war and we were in it to win! Rationing and shortages were soon to follow, as so much was needed for the war: rubber and gasoline to "Keep 'em Rolling" and "Keep 'em Flying", steel and aluminum for building the guns, tanks, planes, ships and trucks we so desperately needed. Whether it was cotton and wool for uniforms, tents and blankets or leather for boots and back packs, the frontline needed it and the homefront provided it! This would be a costly war, not only in terms of human life, but also in hard dollars, so it was "Buy War Bonds and Stamps," and "Save for Victory!".

The Nation needed fighting men and we gave them our sons, husbands and fathers. Our factories needed workers: wives and mothers, sisters and daughters volunteerd, just as they did for the Red Cross, USO and local hospitals. Even our senior citizens went back to work and taught in our schools and watched for enemy aircraft and submarines, taught first aid and patrolled our streets. This was everyone's war.

We may not have been ready for another World War, but it didn't take long for America to mobilize. After their government launched the surprise attack against the U.S. Fleet at Pearl Harbor, Admiral Yamamoto of the Imperial Japanese Navy was right when he said, "I fear we have awakened a sleeping tiger." That sleeping tiger was within months sinking Japan's greatest war ships, knocking "Zeros" out of the sky and dropping bombs on the island of Japan.

We were fighting on two fronts, and it was going to take an equal effort with both in order to achieve our goal. Americans forgot their differences and united against the common enemy, producing more war materials than any other country had ever produced in the shortest period of time: a defiant attitude that was summed up at the time in slogans such as "To hell with Hirohito" and "Back the Attack!" The homefront supported the best trained, best fed, best paid and best cared-for fighting men the world has ever seen. Countless movies have been made on the war, both during it and afterwards, where the villains are defeated and the victorious heroes finally return home to the unsung heroes at home; the task at hand was to make sure it happened for real.

America's Wartime Scrapbook – From Pearl Harbor to V-J Day is a nostalgic, visual look at the cultural ephemera of that era, with all of its brash propaganda and sweet sentimentality. Authors Charles A. Numark and Martin S. Jacobs have collected an astounding array of collectibles which vividly recall American life on the homefront during those chaotic times.

Sixty years ago,
Pearl Harbor awoke to the
screaming of engines and the
sudden savagery of bombs and bullets . . .
a horror that shattered more than the Sunday morning calm; it shook
America out of its complacency and knit the nation into a formidable
power. "Remember Pearl Harbor" became the motto of our war against
Japan and was echoed across the country on almost anything that could
be written on. It was on envelope covers, comic books, window decals,
in newspapers and on posters. The slogan was even emblazoned on dishes
and glasses and banks and toys, plaques and pennants, caps and calendars.
"Remember Pearl Harbor" was everywhere!

5

YOU MUST HELP!

RETAILERS FOR VICTORY
We Are Cooperating

BUY WAR STAMPS
This Store's Best Buy

1942. HARRIS, SEYBOLD, POTTER COMPANY

HE'S WATCHING YOU

NEXT!

JAPAN

6th WAR LOAN

ARE YOU DOING ALL YOU CAN

ATTACK ATTACK ATTACK

BUY WAR BONDS

FLOORED BY THE 7th COLUMN
CARELESSNE

DEFEND AMERICAN FREEDOM
IT'S EVERYBODY'S JOB

1942 NATIONAL ASSOCIATION OF MANUFACTURERS

"Even a little can help a lot - NOW

Buy U.S. WAR STAMPS BONDS

They're fighting harder than ever

are you buying MORE WAR BONDS THAN EVER?

GIVE 'EM BOTH BARRELS

LOOSE LIPS

MIGHT Sink Ships

remember PEARL HARBOR

before it's TOO LATE!

BUY WAR BONDS and STAMPS

TRAIN TO BE A NURSE'S AIDE

BORO CIVILIAN DEFENSE VOLUNTEER OFFICE

keep him off YOUR street!

ROUTE US 50

YOUR WARTIME DUTY! DON'T WASTE WA

DO NOT OPEN FIRE HYDRANTS FOR CHILDREN IN HOT WEATHER

DO SEND THEM TO WADING POOL SHOWERS AT RECREATION CEN

BUY WAR BONDS and STAMPS

CAN... WE WILL.. WE MUST!
Franklin D. Roosevelt

BUY U.S. WAR SAVINGS BONDS & STAMPS NOW

World War II posters helped us mobilize our nation. Inexpensive, accessible, and ever present, the poster was an ideal agent for making war aims the personal mission of every citizen. Government agencies, businesses, and private organizations issued an array of poster images linking the military front with the homefront – calling upon every American to boost production at work and at home.

7

Unconventional in every sense, the purpose of wartime advertising was not to sell, but to boost morale on the homefront and show how even the smallest company and smallest product was vital to the war effort. The text in the ads served up a slice of Americana, reliving when American workers, soldiers and industry pulled together as one, producing more, saving more, and doing more with less.

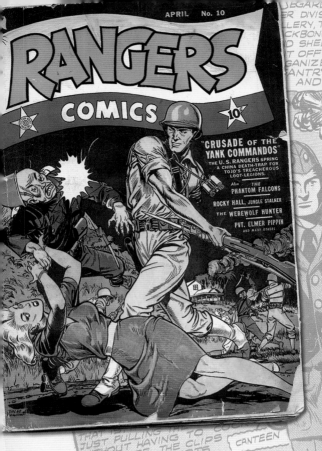

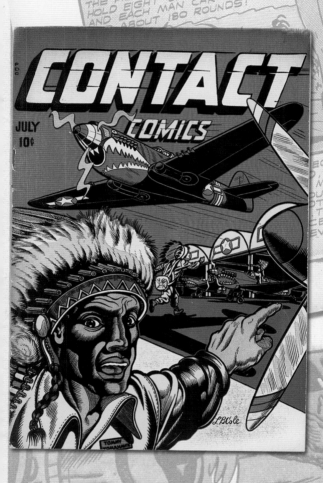

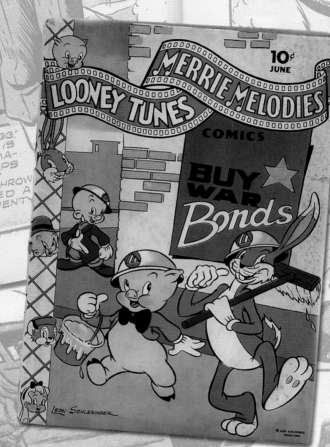

When America went to war, so did comic book characters. Smilin' Jack joined the Army Air Force. Terry fought Japs instead of Pirates. And while Daddy Warbucks served as a general, his adoped daughter, Little Orphan Annie, exhorted real kids to collect scrap metal. However, the most formidable fantasy hero of all, Superman, remained a noncombatant. Super-surprisingly, the man of steel was ruled 4-F by his draft board. His X-ray vision betrayed him. When he took his pre-induction physical early in the war, he was given an eye test; without realizing it he looked right through the eye chart and the wall-to read the letters on another chart in the next room! Rejected, he spent the war pushing the Red Cross and V-bonds.

These patriotic stickers were styled after postage stamps and came in a multitude of sizes and shapes. They were usually lithographed on adhesive paper or made into decals and then stuck to envelopes, stationary, book covers and windows to show support for the war effort.

This Birthday card is bringing
More than a wish or two,
It brings the first installment
On a brand new bond for you.
Each added stamp will do its bit
To push "Mussi" off the map,
Sink the prowling submarines,
And "STAMP" out Hitler and the Jap!

A Very Happy Birthday

VERY HAPPY BIRTHDAY

Best Wishes to You IN THE SERVICE

FRIENDLY GREETINGS for Victory

Keep Smiling at Christmas

Merry Christmas TO A Young American

10¢ WAR STAMP ALBUM
For the purchase of UNITED STATES WAR SAVINGS 10¢ STAMPS

OUR GIFT For Someone In The Service
U·S·A

OKAY YANK—HERE COMES NOTHER TANK!

A-1

RADIOGRAM
IT'S A — Boy
Martin Jacobs
February 23, 1943
MT. Zion Hospital, S.F.

TO SOMEONE in the Service

HAPPY BIRTHDAY TO You

BIRTHDAY Greetings to YOU
IN THE NAVY

WHERE'S THE GARBAGE CAN?

It's your PATRIOTIC DUTY to be my VALENTINE

Patriotic greeting cards were popular on the homefront, and no occasion went unnoticed. Birthday Greetings, Christmas cards, Easter cards, Victory cards – even "Congratulations On Being Drafted" cards – were great morale boosters to the senders and recipients.

The movies of World War II presented a united America facing its enemies who were very real and very determined to win. Most films were fictionalized but based on historical happenings. Between 1941 and 1945, Hollywood produced more than 500 war films. The posters portrayed an image of the war from the Pacific to the battlefields of Europe.

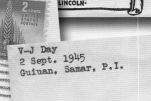

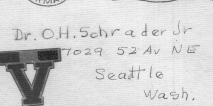

More than 5,000 different envelopes with wartime illustrations and slogans were designed and produced during the war. These ever-popular, and often outlandish covers were used to spread the message of homefront support to our servicemen and women and to each other. They were normally 3″ x 6 3/8″ and up to 3″x 9″. Some of the most prominent cover artists were: W.J. Crosby, L.W. Staehle, Dorothy Knapp, Fluegal, Minkus and others.

One of the most successful advertising tools was the advertising matchbook. The Government and private industry distributed millions of matchbooks with color images that supported the war effort. Every time a match was struck, Americans were reminded that we were at war. Standard matchbook size was $1\frac{3}{8}$" x $4\frac{3}{8}$".

Postcards were churned out at a furious rate to meet the demand during the war. Stores in and around military facilities dutifully dispatched postcards to soldiers, wives, sweethearts, moms and dads, and buddies. Most were linen cards printed in vibrant colors and depicting the 'V' for Victory symbol, Army, Navy, Marine, Air Corps and civilian subjects.

Music sheets were sold with strong cover graphics and war-related titles. Sentimental favorites included 'Remember Pearl Harbor', 'Boogie Woogie Bugle Boy', and the patriotic 'God Bless America'. Photos of composers and recording artists such as Kate Smith, Bing Crosby and Glenn Miller adorned the covers, as well as the hundreds of others who contributed their lyrics to the music sheets.

25

Read the
CLEVELAND PRESS
BEST FOR LIVE SPORTS

Official Score Card and Program

AMERICA'S **NATIONAL** GAME

Watch for Flag on the Terminal Tower

10¢

1944

THE CLEVELAND BASEBALL CO.

ALL-TIME WINNER IN THE REFRESHMENT LEAGUE

Coca-Cola

Refresh Yourself

U.S.

San Francisco **SEALS**
OFFICIAL SCORE BOOK
1943

10¢

Athletics
OFFICIAL SCORE CARD

V

FIRST
Number
1942

VICTORY BOUND!

San Francisco
SEALS
OFFICIAL SCORE BOOK

Seals

International
Baseball

10¢

MAPLE LEAF STAD

SOUTH CAROLINA vs. NORTH CAROLINA
November 4, 1944
KENAN STADIUM   25¢

OFFICIAL
SCORE CARD
SEASON OF 194
PACIFIC COAST LEAGUE

LOS ANGELES BASEBALL CLUB
WRIGLEY FIELD, 435 EAST 42nd PLACE, LOS ANGELES

AUG 13

FOR VICTORY

BUY
WAR
BONDS

47

Phillies

*The Phillies
Pitching for
Uncle Sam.*

10 cents

OFFICIAL **25¢** PROGRAM

OFFICIAL
SCORE CARD   THIRD NUMBER

YOUNG
Guard

PRINCETON — COLUMBIA

1943

Organized sports such
as baseball, football, and boxing never lost their appeal
during the war years. Though star players traded in
their uniforms for military gear, Americans continued
to embrace their favorite recreations during the war
crisis with a trip out to see a ballgame or a prize fight.

26

College of the Pacific
"TIGERS"
vs.
U. S. Navy Pre-Flight School
"AIRDEVILS"
St. Mary's College

Saturday, September 23, 1944
Baxter Stadium, Stockton – 8:00 p. m.
Official Program 10c

1943
WORLD
SERIES
NEW YORK YANKEES
ST. LOUIS CARDINALS

Texas Tech vs
North Texas A. & M.
STADIUM   2:30 P.M.
Price 25c

OFFICIAL AAA PROGRAM
Price 15 cents

THE UNITED WAR FUND

Athletics
OFFICIAL SCORE CARD

WASHINGTON   POLYTECHNIC
vs.   vs.
COMMERCE   LOWELL
FRIDAY, OCTOBER 13, 3:30 P.M.   SATURDAY, OCTOBER 14, 2:30 P.M.

Dartmouth - Coast Guard
November 11, 1944
Official Program   Twenty-five cents

"KEEP 'EM
FLYING"
ARMY and NAVY
NUMBER
10 CENTS

WORLD'S   WORLD'S
CHAMPIONSHIP   CHAMPIONSHIP
GAMES   GAMES
ADMIT ONE
BLEACHER   Sportsman's Park · St. Louis
GAME   RAIN CHECK
1                  $1.15
1942   RETAIN THIS CHECK
NOT GOOD IF DETACHED

BLEACHER
No.
2826

We are now bringing you the 11th annual...
SUGAR BOWL
ALABAMA vs. DUKE
NE STADIUM · JAN
ORLEANS, LA.

OFFICIAL PROGRAM
TWENTY-FIVE CENTS
OCTOBER 21, 1944 - 2:00 P.M. - TAYLOR STADIUM
Alumni Day
LAFAYETTE vs. LEHIGH

Capital Transit Company
On Sundays and
Legal Holidays
two children
under twelve
years of age
may ride free
with pass
bearer
SEPT.
27 to
OCT. 3
1942-INCL.
On Street Car and Bus Lines of Capital Transit Company in the District of Columbia on
fare is 10c or less.
$1.25
WEEKLY
PASS
68843
39

PASADENA ROSE BOWL
FOOTBALL
NEW YEAR'S DAY
JANUARY 1, 1943
2 P.M.
TUNNEL
2
ROW
23
SEAT
118
EST. PRICE $4.00
TAX PAID .40
TOTAL $4.40
SUBJECT TO CONDITIONS ON REVERSE SIDE
1943

27

While Americans kissed their husbands, fathers, sons and daughters good-bye, the war touched everyone – even those who didn't send a loved one overseas. V-Mail, nicknamed 'funny mail' by our troops overseas because of its compact size, became a valuable link between soldiers and their families. The sight most dreaded in any home was a Western Union man or a military officer at the front door. A telegram from the war department was almost never good news. It usually meant a family member was missing in action, captured, wounded or killed.

BLUE BOOK

MAY — 25 CENTS

Stories of adventure for MEN, by MEN

Vengeance in the Night
A novel about the War Dog Battalion and the
Marine Parachute Raiders
by MICHAEL GALLISTER

Foxes Move Fast, *by GORDON KEYNE*
A post-war story of Quest, Inc.

Framed Money... Framed Murder

VOGUE

"United We Stand"

JULY 1, 1942 · PRICE 35 CENTS

FIFTEEN CENTS — JUNE 19, 1944

TIME

THE WEEKLY NEWS MAGAZINE

EISENHOWER
He loosed the fateful lightning.
(World Battlefronts)

VOLUME XLIII

MOVIE-RADIO GUIDE

CENTS · CANADA—12c — PROGRAMS FOR JUNE 14-20

Exclusive!
Truth About Stars

POST

MAY 22, 1943 — 10¢

U. S. NAVY DIVE BOMBER
**How Do the Germans
Feel Now?**
By WERNER KNOP

**We Need a World
Government**

Liberty

MAY 20, 1944 — 10c

Book: DER FUEHRER
Hitler's Rise to Power
SIBERIA

MOVIE-RADIO GUIDE

N CENTS · CANADA—12c — PROGRAMS FOR NOV. 1-7

GENE TIERNEY
See Page 8

This Issue: Intimate Garbo Photo-Story
so: The Brutal Truth About Hollywood Careers

LIFE

U.S. TANK COMMANDER

JULY 22, 1940 — **10** CENTS

Collier's

TEN CENTS
SEPTEMBER 16, 1944

COWARDICE AT CHICAGO
Both Parties Prepare for World
By WENDELL L. WILLI

Americans particularly enjoyed looking through war period magazines with their wonderful ads, stories, photos and illustrations. Some of the most popular periodicals produced during the war were *Readers Digest, Newsweek, LIFE, Saturday Evening Post, TIME, LOOK, Collier's, Liberty, Popular Mechanics, HOLLYWOOD* and pulp-fiction novels.

LOS ANGELES TIMES

THE SPIRIT OF '42

STAMP ALBUM

NORMA KENT OF THE WACS

PUNCH DAVIS OF THE AIRCRAFT CARRIER

A CAMERA TRIP THRO MARCH FIEL

PICTURE BOOK OF THE FIELD AND ITS ACTIVIT

BARRY BLAKE OF THE FLYING FORTRESS

FIGHTI HERO
BATTLE FOR F

Welcome San Francisco Port of Embarkation

CAMP STONEMAN

HomeTown U.S.A

Let's Finish the Job!

VICTORY

Descriptive

WAR FINANCE DIVISION ★ U.S. T

DEAR
FRIEND
PAL
CHUM
SWEETHEART
FUNNY FACE
DADDY

Know your WAR PLANES

The Land of the Free

Supplement to the March, 1943 Reader's Digest
Reproduced by permission from Newsweek Magazine

A POCKET REFERENCE GUIDE
ARMY ★ NAVY
MARINE CORPS
INSIGNIA

STEVE HUNTER of the
U.S. COAST GUARD

CONVOY PATROL
A THRILLING U.S. NAVY STORY

See 'em Move - Just flip the pages

KEEP 'EM FLYING!
U.S.A.

YOU SAID A MOUTHFUL SOLDIER!

ALLEN PIKE of the
PARACHUT SQUAD U.S

WINGS OF THE U.S.A.

THE SECRETS OF RADAR

By "Buck Private" McCollum

With paper a rationed item, the U.S. Government and independent book publishers still produced an abundance of war-related reading books during the war to inspire the fight towards total victory. Through these means, citizens were encouraged to join the civil defense efforts, including homefront volunteer work selling war stamps, bonds and war maps, or booklets on rationing and salvaging scrap.

Patriotism was one thing, but for many a GI, motivation came in the form of the pin-up. Soldiers plastered their lockers, their aircrafts, and even the inside of their helmets with their favorite photos. GIs carried an estimated five million copies of America's favorite pin-up, Betty Grable's famous 'over the shoulder' bathing-suit pose. So famous were the actress's legs that a pair of her used stockings fetched $100,000 in a wartime bond fundraiser. Twentieth Century-Fox then took out an insurance policy with Lloyd's of London, insuring Grable's legs for a million dollars.

Hitler, Tojo and Mussolini were mercilessly ridiculed in the United States. These Axis leaders represented Evil, and gave many American kids nightmares. But the dictators were also a source of ironic amusement, and the humorous, often outlandish cariacatures, never lost their appeal.

Everyone had to live with rationing regulations to offset the wartime food shortages. Saving money and scrap while tending a "Victory garden" for the war effort gave Americans a sense of patriotic duty, and every American made their best effort for the sake of victory. Yet, the main image and symbol of patriotic duty to our country was a red, white and blue rectangular star banner that hung in the front window of an American home to show that a family had a son or daughter in the service.

Civilian defense gave the Americans populace a sense of pride and purpose, with the idea that even on the homefront every man, woman and child could do his or her part for the war effort. While defense savings bonds were developed as part of a plan to help improve the American economy, schools trained future war workers, instructed them in first-aid, assisted in rationing and war-bond sales, organized air-raid, drills, and most of all taught them to be 'good strong Americans'.

42

Aside from the American flag, 'V for Victory' became the most common symbol of commitment to the war effort. The government encouraged families to take the 'V Home Pledge', and urged people of all oppressed nations during World War II to undermine Axis morale by waving two fingers in a V shape. Soon after, the 'V' sign incorporated the Morse code – dot. dot, dot, dash – whose sound meant 'Victory'. This musical message was never decoded by the Germans.

COMPARATIVE TEMPERATURES

	high low		high low
cisco	54 51	Chicago	60 55
	55 51	New Orleans	81 60
o	73 49	New York	— 47
es	67 54	Salt Lake	76 47
	77 —	Washington	77 45

Morning fog;

San Francisco Chronicle
THE CITY'S ONLY HOME-OWNED NEWSPAPER

Chronicle Home Delivery S
Federal war regulations to
rubber prohibit all special deliv
for any reason you do not rece
Chronicle, kindly telephone
1112 or your local Chronicle deale
10 a. m. so the delivery may be
We appreciate your co-operation
emergency.

ED 1865—VOL. CLX, NO. 113   CCCCAAABC

SAN FRANCISCO, TUESDAY, MAY 8, 1945   DAILY 5 CENTS, SUNDAY 15 CENTS

V-E!

VICTORY

San Francisco Examiner
AN AMERICAN PAPER AMERICA FIRST AN AMERICAN N
Monarch of   the Dailies

VOL. CLXXXIII, NO. 46   CCCC✱ 6 A.M. Extra Aug. 15, 1945 Daily and Sunday per Month, $1.75. Daily 5 Cents, Sunday 15 Cents. In Certain Localities Outside Calif., Sunday 25c.

WAR ENDS!

o Sorry, Hirohito Tells Japan

When families were not watching movies or listening to radio broadcasts of our greatest victories, daily accounts of war activities were recounted in daily and Sunday newspapers. Bold headlines depicted our extroadinary exploits, which piled up in quick succession following the attack on Pearl Harbor to the end of the war. Some of the most dramatic war photos and military developments were circulated in the newspapers.

Distinguished combat medals were the highest awards given by the Army, Navy, Air Force and Marines. The fate of a combat soldier was unpredictable. Some served with distinction, performed acts of heroism, endured untold suffering- and emerged with medals of bravery. Unit patches and insignias came in a variety of sizes. They were worn by servicemen and adorned the shoulders of their service uniforms, while Squadron patches were colorful and comical, designed to boost morale or scare the enemy.

Douglas MacArthur was one of America's most brilliant generals, and commanded the US Army forces in the Pacific. Together with Admiral Chester Nimitz, he developed and perfected the strategy of 'island hopping', bypassing enemy strongholds in the Pacific, cutting off the garrison's supplies and conquering the Japanese. MacArthur also directed the Japanese surrender on the deck of the battleship USS Missouri, in Tokyo Bay in September 1945.

KEEP OLD GLORY FLYING.

Gen. Douglas MacArthur

GEN. DOUG. MacARTHUR

MacArthur's Address to Congress

April 19. 1951   Washington. D. C.

DON'T LET GENERAL MacARTHUR DOWN—
BUY WAR BONDS!

The Timken Roller Bearing Company, Canton, Ohio

War toys and games were plentiful during the war and were very popular with American children.

Colorful and inexpensive, they were an ideal medium for recreation and delivering messages to kids about America's role in the war. The majority of the toys and games were made from non-strategic materials such as wood, cardboard, plastic and cloth. Boys were kept busy building airplane models, tanks and jeeps, fighting the Germans and Japanese, while girls played Army-Navy Red Cross nurses with paper-doll cut-outs and assembled picture-puzzles of soldiers and sailors.

A valued treasure on the homefront was ladies' sweetheart jewelry – not because of its intrinsic value – but because of its great importance to the war effort. To wear a piece of patriotic jewelry was to tell the world you cared. Sweetheart jewelry included pins, lockets, wings, necklaces, pendants, earrings, bracelets and rings and were a great source of support on the homefront.

FLYING CADETS

Coloring Book

PB2Y-2 NAVY
PATROL BOMBER

B-17 ARMY
FLYING FORTRESS

F4U-1
NAVY FIGHTER

A-17A ARMY
ATTACK BOMBER

F4F-3
NAVY FIGHTER

P-38
ARMY
FIGHTER

SB2C-1
NAVY DIVE
BOMBER

P-39
AIRACOBRA

P-47
ARMY PURSUIT

BEAUTIFUL BOOKS FOR CHILDREN

the MERRILL
PUBLISHING COMPANY
CHICAGO

P-40 ARMY
FIGHTER

During the war, Amusement Park concessionaires managed games of chance and skill and offered prizes of painted chalk, resin, porcelain, or plaster statues pasted with glitter depicting Uncle Sam, soldiers, sailors, marines, aviators, nurses, eagles, even savings banks. Later, these fun-looking novelties were often found in homes standing on top of the mantel piece or the family console radio.

or mothers and family members at home, the
uvenir 'pillow cover' was a fond reminder that
eir sons and daughters were close to their
earts. Servicemen bought the covers, usually
ade of silk and mailed them back home. They
owed patriotism in a variety of ways, includ-
g the colorful scarves and handkerchiefs
mericans wore with their clothing.

LIFE

AN ACE IN THE HOLE

MANIFOLD PRESSURE

JANUARY 30, 1939 10 CE

Some of the greatest dramas of World War II occurred in the skies, where our courageous and tenacious fighter pilots flew propeller-driven aircrafts and battled in dogfights with the enemy. The fighter planes were our salvation, but it was the bombers alone that provided victory in the Pacific and Europe. During the war, America produced over 300,313 aircraft and trained more than one million aircrew to man them. The majority of the pilots were young – often too young to vote for their government – but not too young to die for our country.

Billams

ME

PLATOON
CO A·29·BATTALION
1815

Sincere best wishes
Mickey Rooney

LTJG Alex Vracin
VF-16
19 Victories

While millions of Americans kissed their husbands, fathers, sons and daughters good-bye, the war touched everyone, including those left behind on the homefront. A snapshot photo of men in uniform would be sent to loved ones, and they became a cherished symbol of the victorious heroes.

CHRONOLOGY OF WAR EVENTS

War in the Pacific:

- December 7, 1941 Japanese fighter planes, torpedo bombers and dive-bombers swoop down at Pearl Harbor, Hawaii and other naval and military installations on the island of Oahu, bombing, torpedoing, and strafing.
- The United States officially declares war on Japan on December 8, 1941.
- General Douglas MacArthur is appointed commander-in-chief of the Southwest Pacific.
- On December 12, Colin Kelly, America's named first war hero, dies a hero's death. He is the country's first Medal of Honor winner.
- On April 18, 1942, Lt. James Doolittle leads the surprise attack on Tokyo, Japan, from the aircraft carrier Hornet. This is considered America's first major moral victory and revenge of Pearl Harbor.
- On November 14, 1942, the cruiser USS Juneau, carrying the five Sullivan brothers, is hit and sunk at the battle of Guadalcanal. The Navy awards posthumous Purple Heart to the brothers, and christens a new destroyer, USS Sullivan's in their honor.
- The Battle of the Coral Sea, a naval battle fought entirely with aircraft, is a major victory for the Allies in the war, costing the Japanese seven warships and one carrier.
- Allied victories are scored at the Battle of Midway, Guadal-canal, Tarawa, Iwo Jima, Okinawa, and at the Battle of Leyte Gulf.

War in Europe:

- On December 11, 1941, the United States declares war on Germany and Italy.
- In July of 1943 the Allies invade Sicily, which surrenders on September 30, 1943.
- On December 24, 1943, General Dwight D. Eisenhower is chosen Supreme Commander of the Allied Expeditionary Forces.
- June 6, 1944, otherwise known as D-Day, involves an all-out attack against the enemy with three million fighting men landing at Omaha, Gold, Juno and Sword, France's Normandy coast beaches.
- French and U.S. troops liberate Paris on August 25, 1944.
- The Germans ultimately give in to the Allied forces. Mussolini is captured and hung. Adolf Hitler and his mistress, Eva Braun, commit suicide on May 1, 1945.
- On May 7, Germany surrenders unconditionally to the Allies after almost six years of war.
- President Truman proclaims May 8 V-E Day to honor the victory in Europe.
- On August 6, 1945, the first atom bomb falls on the city of Hiroshima, Japan.
- On August 9, 1945, a second atomic bomb is dropped on Nagasaki, Japan.
- Japan surrenders to the Allies on August 14, 1945, or V-J Day.
- On September 2, 1945, aboard the battleship U.S.S. Missouri in Tokyo Bay, in the presence of Emperor Hiroito, a Japanese representative signs the unconditional surrender agreements with Fleet Chester W. Nimitz and General Douglas MacArthur. The war is officially over.

7th
WAR LOAN

NOW·· ALL TOGETHER

63

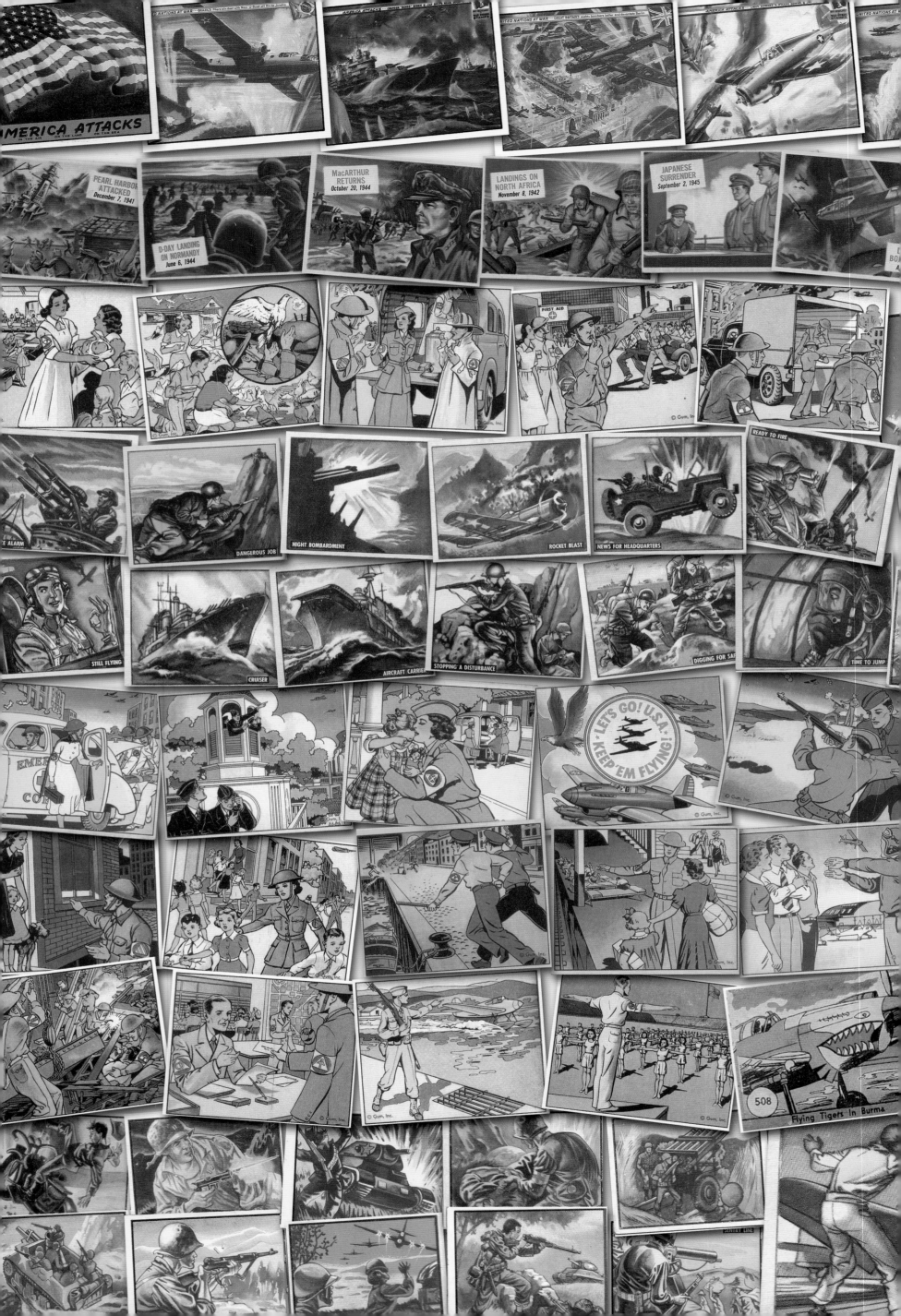